"The performer's mind"

Bianca Fenn

This is an IndieMosh book
brought to you by MoshPit Publishing
an imprint of Mosher's Business Support Pty Ltd

PO Box 147
Hazelbrook NSW 2779

indiemosh.com.au

Copyright © Bianca Fenn 2017

The moral right of the author has been asserted in accordance with the Copyright Amendment (Moral Rights) Act 2000.

All rights reserved. Except as permitted under the Australian Copyright Act 1968 (for example, fair dealing for the purposes of study, research, criticism or review) no part of this publication may be reproduced, stored in a retrieval system, or transmitted in any form or by any means, electronic, mechanical, photocopying, recording or otherwise, without the written permission of the publisher.

Cataloguing-in-Publication entry is available from the National Library of Australia: http://catalogue.nla.gov.au/

Title:	The Performer's Mind
Author:	Fenn, Bianca (1984–)
ISBNs:	978-1-925666-78-6 (paperback)
	978-1-925666-79-3 (ebook – epub)
	978-1-925666-80-9 (ebook – mobi)

The author has made every effort to ensure that the information in this book was correct at the time of publication. However, the author and publisher accept no liability for any loss, damage or disruption incurred by the reader or any other person arising from any action taken or not taken based on the content of this book. The author recommends seeking third party advice and considering all options prior to making to decisions or taking action in regard to the content of this book.

Cover artwork by Jacqui Lewis, www.khokhoart.com

Cover design by Ditta Prawiro

To my balanced, calm and stable husband.

Contents

PREFACE vii
CHAPTER ONE 1
  Confidence
CHAPTER TWO 5
  Preparation
CHAPTER THREE 8
  Fame
CHAPTER FOUR 12
  Perspective
CHAPTER FIVE 15
  Feelings
CHAPTER SIX 19
  Judgement
CHAPTER SEVEN 22
  Identity
CHAPTER EIGHT 25
  Perfectionism
CHAPTER NINE 29
  Vision

PREFACE

Each moment in life is a lesson to learn, each breath is valuable and every word in this book is destined to be read by you. Yep - I'm one of those odd balls that believes in a purpose and a path for each of us. I have absolutely no doubt you are reading this book because you need to.

Do you ever feel consumed by self-doubt and disabled by insecurity? This little book is based on things that have helped me through my own battles and those of my singing students. It is here to help performers but is relevant for anyone who needs to perform in any capacity of life; parents, teachers, managers, students.... humans. This book is especially for those who feel the desire, the push or pull of needing more from life. It's for those people who know they could do more than they currently are, if only they could get past that thing that is holding them back.

Have you asked for help only to be greeted with gentle encouragement and a sweet voice of a loved one, telling you, "You'll be fine"? Do you recognise you need a kick up the butt, you need to face the reality of the issues that are holding you back so you can move past this awkward stage? This book details some fairly obvious truths that can often be forgotten and also some different thoughts for you to consider in the most direct fashion possible. The aim of this book is to get to the point quickly, give you alternative ways to view your situation and then encourage you to get on with it so you don't waste any more of your precious and limited time on this earth.

I am a singing teacher - not super qualified to comment on the mind, but I felt compelled to write this book. I've tested these words with many different people who have varying levels of emotional dependancy, performance anxiety and fear and I have seen the difference they have made. If I could help you too, why wouldn't I?

I hope you can see my motivation and feel my loving care. I don't profess to have all the answers. In fact - I'm the first to admit my shortcomings, which contributes to why I can comment on this topic. Writing this book is evidence of how I always aim to practice what I preach.

I want to encourage you to question everything you have ever read and been told in life including what's in this book. I challenge you to test it out by making some changes. And in return, I believe your life will develop, your performances will flourish and you will achieve what you are meant to achieve in your life. You'll become a person of influence and an inspiration for those in your world as you step into your full potential.

CHAPTER ONE
Confidence

The age old question; What came first? The chicken or the egg? Or more importantly for the purpose of this book; What came first? The confidence or the challenge?

I regularly hear the excuse, "I'm just not confident enough." If you have ever found yourself saying those words, I want you to question yourself. How do *you* think confidence develops? Is it something you live without one day, have a really good night's sleep and then wake up with the next day? Is it connected to your iron level or the amount of nutrients you consume? Do you believe confidence kicks in at a certain age or do you think you are born with it? Please take a moment to question and clearly develop your own opinion about this matter.

I believe confidence is developed once you know you can do something and I think the only way to truly know if you can do something is by trying to do it and then succeeding at it. Confidence can be encouraged by kind words of those you allow to speak into your life or by choosing to focus on the positives of the experience and the things that went well. Confidence can be developed by setting realistic expectations and meeting them. Confidence can often grow with age

Chapter One: Confidence

because opportunities present themselves over the years and repetition allows the proof of ability to surface.

I do understand, the response and encouragement (or lack thereof) from our parents can help or hinder the initial level of confidence we carry through our developing years. But, when does your life become your own? When will you realise your parents were only doing what they could? They themselves may have been battling with their own lack of confidence and accidentally or deliberately transferred it onto you. I don't know your personal story, but most of the sad stories I've heard of parents screwing with their kids' heads - came out of human error. Yep, the same or similar human errors that we are making today. We need to break out of the belief that parents are perfect, that they are responsible for the shape of our lives. I recognise this is a very narrow view of some pretty complex issues, but without the time to explore this further, the core of the truth I am trying to project is that parents aren't always right. Parents get it really wrong sometimes. That doesn't mean we need to follow in their footsteps or allow their crap to hinder our gold.

Try to trade your language. Swap the word *confidence* for the word *courage* and see if you continue to speak the same way. Instead of "I'm just not confident enough" it would become "I'm just not courageous enough." Would you be proud of that reasoning? Does that still sound like an acceptable excuse? As fairytales have taught us, courage is essential in achievement. Courage is a moment of choice, a decision to do what needs to be done despite the risk.

There are countless stories of courage based on life or death situations. They don't seem as relevant for a book about performance but it is the same choice to be courageous that propelled the soldier, Desmond Doss to rescue 75 men (one at a time while under fire, without carrying a weapon) that stands up for someone who is being picked on, asks someone on a date, chooses to leave a job or apply for a promotion, tries out a different style of cuisine, makes a presentation at work, rocks up to that audition or steps out on that stage.

Notice how an outsider may perceive someone as confident when they are in fact courageous.

We have discussed that confidence is being sure that you can do something. Courage is acting on it even if you don't know you can do it. Courage is acting without being assured of success. Taking a risk.

If confidence was necessary to achieve, I'm fairly sure the world would be full of ... well, not much. People would be waiting until they were guaranteed success, *before* they attempted anything new or challenging. There is no such guarantee in life. I know the thought of risk can be daunting. We can get so hung up on the possibility of it not working that we get confused and form the opinion that it *will* go wrong. I want you to change your thinking and ask yourself - what if it didn't go wrong? What if it worked? What if you *did* do it?

People often treat a lack of confidence like an illness or something that has been unfairly given to them to live with, so therefore it is their reason for not getting things done in their life. Nope! I'm calling it. That's not true. It's up to *you* whether you take up opportunities to develop confidence through courageous choices, trying things and potentially succeeding. Erase the 'no confidence' excuse from your book of reasons why sitting and settling is your future.

Another misunderstanding I have observed is that people get "*humble*" confused with "*insecure*" and "*confidence*" confused with "*cocky*." Maybe it's the Australian culture I have grown up in, but often the "real bloody legends" are the ones who struggle and strive, the victims, the "underdog", certainly not the "tall poppy" or the success story. In this culture we are so cautious of sounding "up ourselves" that we do the opposite and talk about ourselves in a manner that we would not accept from a stranger. As we invest in this language, we speak the same dialogue with our internal voice which then transfers into thoughts and before we know it, our beliefs and actions reflect this bull. I get it, it's hard to go against the grain and to challenge this culture - but it's not getting you anywhere.

You might just have to try to do things differently to allow yourself to be a success at the risk of potentially failing or being perceived as cocky.

CHAPTER TWO
Preparation

I love stationary. I love, love, love stationary. I also love being organised and writing lists. I have lists of lists. I love the feeling of being in control and knowing how everything will work. I love planning. It makes me feel like I am "on top of life" and that I know what to expect.

My husband is definitely not a list-writer. In fact, I think he finds it funny. He'll stumble across a list every now and again and mock me because I had written a list that started with some of the basics. Eg. Tuesday. Shower - Breakfast - Get dressed. He thinks lists are just to remind me of stuff and so doesn't understand how I could forget to be clean, fed or clothed. What he doesn't realise is, I have probably memorised the entire list including all the tiny details of things that need to be done that day that he always forgets! Writing lists is not to do with memory, it's to do with preparation and getting a clear idea of my day so I can live it efficiently.

I recognise my list writing is slightly over the top. I often find myself wasting time writing lists when I could just be getting stuff done! I also recognise that someone who is qualified on personality types would describe me as a control freak. I do find security in

Chapter Two: Preparation

controlling my day, in planning what is going to happen and in having everything run smoothly. I'm not silly though, I have learnt that no matter how many lists I write, the day doesn't always end up following my plan. Often, to my horror, I don't get to tick everything off my list and other things pop up.

Flexibility is just as valuable as preparation. Whoah!!! I said it. I'm still not sure I believe it, but I'll just keep writing and see if I can convince myself. To be able to adapt in any situation is extremely important. To be in the moment, to think in the present or to have problem-solving common sense is what helps us get through the tough times. Now, I'm not saying to my students that you can get away without preparation. Preparation is under-rated. When you are practiced, prepared and organised, you are much better equipped to face the challenge. Practice really does make perfect... until something goes wrong.

In terms of performance, I can practice and practice and practice (which I do and I think you should too) and I can feel in control but then on the day, I can wake up with a cough or during the performance a phone can ring or a baby can cry and AHHHH - that wasn't part of my plan! There is such a thing as being too prepared, too stuck, too in-flexible.

When performing live with other musicians, things happen. Wrong notes are played, errors are made, lyrics are forgotten - we are human after all. When these things occur, we can get hung up on the mistake, stuck in the past. We can get so distracted from what we're currently trying to deliver that it can then all fall apart.

For example, Verse 1 goes well, the Chorus is fine but in Verse 2 we fumble over a forgotten lyric. Instead of focussing on the next chorus, we get stuck in Verse 2 - beating ourselves up over how we screwed it up. So rather than holding the song together and continuing through the tune (which would then override the mistake in Verse 2) every section of the tune from that point on is a mess. Sometimes we cry or run off the stage, freeze or laugh. However we survive that moment, we definitely ruin any chance of a performance we were hoping for. Often these experiences then stay with us and we carry around the hurtful memory which can stop us from stepping up on that stage again.

To come in knowing what you need to do is excellent, to expect everything to go to plan is unrealistic. Go with the flow, be mindful, actively listen, be in the moment, participate, problem-solve, choose and then let it go.

Mistakes can often be highlights. I think of performances I've seen. I know the lyrics off by heart, the singer stuffed them up but came up with a cover. I find it even more impressive than if they didn't have the challenge to overcome! As an audience member, that moment wakes me up!

I went along to a school production to watch one of my students perform. Everyone was doing a really great job, very professional, really well rehearsed. Then someone dropped a prop, someone got the giggles and someone had to improvise and cover up the incident. The audience burst into laughter! That was the most memorable part of the show - I would even say, the highlight. The magic that was created in that moment could not be planned for.

To be prepared is a great thing, but to be stuck in your plans is not.

CHAPTER THREE
Fame

First of all, let's get one thing clear about fame - to be famous does not mean everyone loves you. Yes, lots of people may - but there's most likely a similar portion of people who don't. If you have found yourself wanting to be famous; needing the attention of the masses - ask yourself, what do you think will improve with fame?

One thing that really helped me deal with the desire and disappointment in people pleasing was the realisation that it doesn't matter how "good" I am - there will always be varied opinions and aesthetic biases. Even if I have perfect pitch and choose the sound of every note I sing, some people will still not like it. The minute I realised that, I felt a freedom! The aim of my game shifted from trying to please everyone to trying to find out exactly what I like.

Life is full of good and bad, ups and downs, heroes and villains and so there is no denying that the life we live is one of contrast. I've never heard of someone who has loved every day of their life or who escaped life's challenges. It's the low points that make us realise the high ones! It's the struggles that help us appreciate the victories! It's our differences that encourage us to explore and try new things! To hope every opinion of you will be positive is completely unrealistic. Just like you have some things you don't like, other people can too! How exhausting it would be to have to justify every preference we had?

First, we need to acknowledge we do have preferences; due to our environment or DNA or whatever, we lean towards some things more than others - we prefer particular colours, tastes, clothes, music. In saying we prefer something, we acknowledge we like some things more than others - which means, there are some things we don't like as much (if at all!). Do we need to justify every preference? No way! So why do we feel upset when there are people who don't prefer the way we do things? Chances are, you probably don't like the way they do things either, so who really cares?

Remember the old saying, "Fame is fleeting". People's approval will come and go. Seasons change as do preferences. What people think is "hot" one year, they may cast aside as "old or "out-of-date" the next. How often do we ask "what happened to so and so?" and "where are they now?" We need to recognise our self worth is not determined by people's opinion or view of us. If we don't, we fall into the trap of needing people to like us for us to like ourselves.

You are more than what people think of you.

Amy, Prince, Michael, Elvis and Whitney all have a few things in common, but the most obvious one would be - they are no longer with us. That's right - famous people don't live forever. They are not immune from physical or mental illness, age.... life! Having lots of people know your name and what you do for a living, makes no difference to the amount of lives you live.

Chapter Three: Fame

Our society paints a very pretty picture of famous people. They have heaps of money that they spend however they like, making their lives very comfortable. They have assistance in developing and preserving their physical beauty, they're usually fit and healthy and have plenty of time to keep their calories and thoughts in order. They have families who are taken care of. They live the best possible looking life, so therefore, they are happy!

But we know that's not the full story yeah? Yes, they may have money, but anyone who has had money realises that it's never enough - we all want more. They may get to wear the latest fashion and have regular beauty treatments, but their internal organs will age just like ours! They may have access to the latest fitness gear and the best personal trainers, but they still have to sweat! They may have assistance with cooking healthy meals, but they still have to turn down the bag of chips. Their families may be taken care of, but they still fight about stupid little things. They may even be happy a lot of the time, but they still have days where they feel sad. They still feel pressured, stressed, tired, disappointed, hungry, fat and sick. No-one is immune from life.

Fame will not make you any more happy than you are right now.

Now let's discuss ability. Do you think famous people are famous because they are the best at their thing? Fame is a bit of a mystery. Why are some people famous and others are not? Sometimes people do anything to get in the spotlight, even if it means ruining their reputation. I've heard it said, "all exposure is good exposure." Really?!?!? Yep, you'll get people talking about you but I promise, it's not always going to be conversations you'd want to hear.

I'll use Miley Cyrus as an example but this formula of fame has been tried and tested throughout the ages. Controversial statements, outfits, attitudes - shocking the "general public" (non famous people) to get attention. Miley Cyrus has become less about her singing and more about her hair cut, tattoos and sex life. Does that mean that as her fame increased, her ability also improved? Nope. It just meant more people were judging her. She became less about her as a person, a musician and turned into Miley the product - the disposable product.

Being famous at any level, doesn't make you better at your craft. You're just famous.

Now for some controversy! Do you think doctors are better people than teachers? Do you think lawyers are better people than cleaners? Do you think boys are better than girls? Do you think young people are better than old people? Do you think white people are better than black people? Do you think famous people are better than un-knowns? Or, do you think everyone is equal? This is a huge topic. If you do think some people are better than others, can I ask you to question why? What is it that makes one person 'better' than the other?

Is the rich, famous, "good looking" rock-star who cheats on his wife more prestigious and a "better person" than the father who lives in a third world country, who owns nothing, who is an unknown and who has battled to keep his family safe and healthy? I can't answer these questions for you, but I have a clear opinion.

Being famous does not make you a better person.

CHAPTER FOUR

Perspective

My friend Simone is one of the nicest people in the world, the definition of sweet and an incredible singer. We used to sing together a lot and recently, we were asked to sing for a friend's wedding ceremony. I instantly wanted to reply no. I mean, I wanted to sing with her and I wanted to sing for them if they wanted me to, but I couldn't believe they would actually want me to. I thought perhaps they thought they should ask me. The friends who were getting married are two of the most capable musicians in Melbourne and so I knew the wedding guests would most likely be amazing musicians too. The thought of performing in front of them intimidated me.

After giving it much thought and talking to my husband, I decided I should say yes. My reasoning was - if they actually did want me to sing and I said no, they could be upset about it and it could draw attention to myself (which I would never want), but if I said yes and they didn't want me to do it, well they couldn't exactly get upset with me because they asked me to! I was however, freaking out. I didn't think I sounded good singing the songs and I knew with the nerves I'd be battling, my voice and mind would need some serious control which I doubted I would be able to settle in the moment.

It was time for the run through, Simone and I met with the guitarist and played through the songs. She was so gracious and completely un-phased by the thought of who would be listening to us. Her focus was not on herself but wanting to do her best for our friends who were getting married. The day was about them after all. Well... I felt like a fool. Who was I to think people would be focusing on me? The day had nothing to do with me!

Time and time again, I hear students freak themselves out over performance opportunities. "Should I? Shouldn't I?" There are those who usually turn them down because they are worried they'll fail. They're concerned they'll make mistakes and their reputations will be ruined or they'll have a negative impact on the event and let everyone down. Sometimes I just want to tell them - no one actually cares whether you do this or not. It doesn't really matter - no one cares about it as much as you do. You'll be the only one that misses out.

It's up to us if we want to take up challenges, gain experiences, grow and stretch. If we don't, no one else really cares. You may be lucky enough to have loved ones who really believe in you and want to see more from you, but if you don't do it - it's not going to mean their life stops or even pauses. They'll keep living.

I'm one of those crazy people who finds comfort in realising how unimportant I am. Some people need to feel needed, irreplaceable, unforgettable... me on the other hand, I love knowing that no matter what I do - no matter how many mistakes I make, the world will continue to turn and life will just keep on moving. When I get overwhelmed by life's crazy demands, I remove myself from my normal routine and I escape.

Chapter Four: Perspective

I love the river, I love layers of land, hills, trees.... nature, so I take myself somewhere huge and I sit there and focus on the enormity of the universe. I focus on my small-ness and the greatness I'm surrounded by and I remember that my issue is not such a big deal. I reflect on my past and the countless times I've been caught up with things I thought were life or death situations and I actually struggle to remember them. I then focus on some of the little things; leaves, ants and whatever else is on the ground and I remind myself that the whole time that ant was born and was living its life - I kept living mine completely unaware of it.

Perspective is one of the best things you can give yourself in moments when you feel like everything is about you. It's not all about you. It's really not. Everyone has their own stuff to deal with and everyone is just trying to do the best they can. They really don't care about your gig as much as you think they do. But.... you care about it.

Don't rob yourself of opportunities for fear of getting it wrong. Give yourself the chance to live your life - the one that matters to you.

CHAPTER FIVE
Feelings

How important are your feelings to you?

I feel a lot. I'm one of those people who experience every possible emotion all within the hour. I cry when watching movies, listening to music and when I'm tired. I get angry when my computer is being stupid, when I hear of something unjust and when I've got PMS. I laugh when my husband dances and when other people laugh. I also feel tired, nervous, rested, scared, exhausted, ready, anxious, depressed, confident, insecure, excited, hopeful, strong and weak. I feel it all. It changes, very frequently. Sometimes I can figure out why I feel the way I do, other times I can't. Sometimes my emotions make sense, other times they don't. Sometimes I can hold it in, sometimes I have to let it out. Sometimes I blame others, sometimes I take responsibility for them. Sometimes I love the way I feel, sometimes I hate it.

From my understanding, I'm not the only one who goes through this daily. So, if this is the case. How important are your feelings to you? Do they even matter?

I have discovered that I can't make decisions based on my feelings. If I did what I felt like doing, I would be extremely obese. I always feel like eating! I would

Chapter Five: Feelings

never get out of bed before midday. I would rarely go to work, do the grocery shopping, cook, exercise, clean, wash my hair, floss, wash my bedding, do the dishes, take out the rubbish. I definitely would never have opened the music school or written this little book.

Fear is a feeling. Fear is not a reality. Fear cannot stop you from doing things.... if you do things. Fear cannot hurt you, unless you allow it to disable you. Being scared is part of being human. Being scared of things can protect us from danger, it can help you make decisions that are good for you, but it can also contribute to decisions that give you a boring life. There's a fine line between safe and boring, dangerous and adventurous.

Happiness is not a goal. You cannot seriously expect to live each day happily. I'm a realist when it comes to things like this. If you're happy when someone close to you dies, I think you're warped. I recognise you can focus on the good things from a life well lived, or you could find peace in the fact they are no longer suffering, you could even feel relief - but, happy? That doesn't sit right with me. Bad things will happen to you, not because you deserve it, but because we live in a world where bad things happen!

I think it's ok to be sad. Often people deny themselves the full palette of emotions because they think to be sad is to be negative and no-one likes a "Negative Nancy!" If you feel sad sometimes, you don't need to bash yourself up about it. It's perfectly normal and healthy. Sad is an important emotion, it plays a part in life. It's not your life, it isn't who you are, it doesn't define what you can or can't do, it's just something you need to feel sometimes.

Actions are like hot chips and feelings are like gravy. Sometimes feelings can enhance the experience, they can help make things extra tasty, but you don't need to have the gravy to eat the chips. I don't have to feel happy in order to get on with my life. I don't have to feel brave in order to try something. I don't have to feel strong before I test my strength and pick up a heavy box. I don't have to feel excited to experience good things. Feelings just come along for the ride as we live our life. Don't give them too much power. Don't allow your feelings to guide your steps and your future.

Feeling nervous, is a feeling. Being nervous is completely normal and ok. Being nervous can make the performance even more rewarding, the relief of completing the task is satisfying. Nerves get the blood pumping and make you feel a world of weird things in your tummy and knees and hands and arm pits. It's all part of the experience! To feel nervous does not mean you can't pull it off, it just means that when you do, you'll feel awesome. If for whatever reason you don't, you'll feel like crap. But once again, it doesn't change anything. Feeling awesome or feeling crap are both just feelings.

Sometimes people believe "feelings" and "intuition" are the same thing. They make decisions "following their gut" about something. Let's clarify what I mean with these words. I believe intuition is that little quiet inner voice that guides you towards doing what is right, or that you ignore when you do something wrong. It whispers in your ear and encourages you to try new things, it gives you desires and dreams. Feelings are then what jump in the way, feelings are often really loud and obnoxious. Feelings make you think you can't do it.

If you live your life based on feelings that come and go, that are unreliable and always changing. Your life will be unstable and your progress will be slow because

Chapter Five: Feelings

you'll take one step forward, one back and one to the side. Keep stepping forward no matter how you feel. Your feelings will follow.

CHAPTER SIX

Judgement

My sister has always been my idol. She's 10 years older than me, but we act as if we're no more than 2 years apart. I can remember when she first needed to wear glasses, I thought she was so beautiful and looked so cool, I convinced my teacher and my Mum that I needed to go get my eyes tested too. I would have done anything to be like her, even if glasses didn't help! She's reliable, humble, loyal, loving and intelligent or like one of the lines in my cross-stitch acrostic gift for her spelled out "intellect" (yes, it didn't make sense in my crafty gift either.)

Unfortunately, my sister has been cheated on numerous times by her ex-partners. One of the most exhausting tests she endured in those relationships, was how her partners would doubt her honesty. They were jealous and would often ask if she was cheating on them. My sister's response was always a definite "no", but she would never think to ask them the same question back because it hadn't even entered her mind as a possibility. In her head, she had no reason to doubt them whereas the cheaters seemed to be filtering their thoughts and words through their own deceit. They were wearing their "cheaters glasses" and all they could see was other people acting the same as them.

I recognise this won't apply to everyone, but it really helped me to challenge my assumptions of the audience. Sometimes we can assume people find it amusing to see us fail. We can think people are focussing on our mistakes or the things that go wrong. We can think the audience is assessing us, judging us and comparing us to others. Now - why do we think that? Is it actually because we, ourselves do that when listening to someone else sing, or watch them make that presentation or run that meeting? Or is it because we hear others around us passing judgement? Do we hang out with people who fall into the trap of commenting on all the things the performer could be doing differently?

To be honest, I have. I have a history of tearing people to shreds on TV who dress inappropriately or make terrible hair-do choices and I often feel the need to comment on famous singers who don't sing things the way I would. I have noticed with time that these comments and thoughts don't help much. They don't influence the person who is living life as best as they can on TV, they prove nothing about my own ability or how well I'm doing and the impact it has on those around me is definitely not a positive one (no one would want to watch a reality singing competition show with me!) How do my comments impact me? I get frustrated, annoyed and drained in the moment but the lasting effects are so much worse. When I perform, I often judge myself as harshly as I judge others. I've opened up that "negative, judgemental, not good enough" sphere, where no one is capable of succeeding - including me. So how on earth could I expect to feel excited about a performance or feel good about what I had done?

In changing the way we listen to or watch others, in choosing to focus on the positives in those we observe, we create a shift in our mind that can then allow us to see positives in ourselves and release us from the trick of the lie that tells us everyone thinks poorly of us. When we can move away from these habitual, exhausting judgements - we begin to feel free of not being judged ourselves. I'm not saying there won't be people watching you who do judge you, I'm just saying that you'll start to view those people differently - taking away their power and recognising they are actually the ones who are imprisoning themselves by their judgements of you.

This change is a really active one. When you are watching someone do their thing, be deliberate about your thoughts. Assess what is going on in your mind. If it's a judgement you wouldn't want to hear someone has made about you, replace it with a positive thought instead and then meditate on it. Perhaps you could go a step further, and action a compliment. Go up to that person or post about how well they did with that positive thought you were focussing on. You will not only start to invest your energy into shifting the culture, you will start to feel free from judgement yourself.

CHAPTER SEVEN
Identity

Who are you?!?!?!

Who you are is not defined by who you think you *should* be, or who *others* think you should be. Who you are will always be an evolving project, a work in progress, a developing film. With time, experience (good and bad), the picture of who you are becomes clearer and clearer. Who I was, is not who I am and it's definitely not who I am going to be. This process is the same for everyone who wants to become better. Every person is in a different stage of their development. It's not based on age, location, vocation, sex or status. Each story is completely unique and each journey moves at its own pace.

Comparisons are a waste of energy. Trying to be like someone else is pointless. That person already exists, so to be a duplicate (not even the original), will lessen your value and won't get you anywhere. The English cleric, writer and collector Colton originally said, "Imitation is the sincerest form of flattery." What Colton forgot to add in was... imitators are really annoying. Like honestly - sweat, tears, trials and sacrifice have been poured into creating the original. To copy it is nothing but lazy. If you do copy others because you like what they have done, I challenge you to pay your compliments in another way!

To be influenced is fine. I have been positively influenced by those I admire. I have figured out what I respect about the characters around me (and what I don't). I have learnt from others mistakes and successes, but to directly copy someone or hope to *be* them is a very different beast. Don't get carried away.

Jealousy is definitely a human default. Whenever we struggle with something and we see someone else who doesn't, it's understandable to wish to be in their position. To stew on these things, to focus on other peoples victories without knowing the full story of how they got there is foolish. As I mentioned in the chapter *Fame*, we know and can recognise that life is full of ups and downs. Everyone's life - not just yours. You may not see the downs portrayed on that person's Instagram account or in your Facebook newsfeed, but that doesn't mean they didn't cry and nearly die creating that life, that concept or that idea.

Theft is shocking. Our music school is in an industrial estate which we share with a bunch of tradies including a mechanic friend. He's an absolute legend of a bloke. Quiet, unassuming and extremely hard working. He's been through his fair share of struggles; from going through a divorce to getting a mystery illness that knocked him out for too long and what makes it all even worse is, his business was robbed. Not once, but twice, while he was going through all of this. His computers, money and cars were stolen from his property in the middle of the night. The thought of someone breaking into his successful business and taking what he had worked so hard for, devastated me. Perhaps because it was so close to home or because I cared about him or perhaps because it's just so obviously wrong. Anyone who becomes a thief is

Chapter Seven: Identity

desperate. They aren't considering the person they are stealing from. They are most definitely not leaving a positive mark on the world.

Imitation is flattery, but to be honest - I don't really care if people want what I have. That doesn't make me feel any better about myself. If people could see the sacrifice it has taken to build our business, I could guarantee they wouldn't want it. So to know people want the results of the hard work I have put in, is no shock - of course they do!

Remind yourself, someone else's success does not equate to your failure. Or - someone else's failure will not make you more successful. Other people can look beautiful at the same time as you! This world is so big, there is enough opportunity for everyone.

Don't be a try-hard. Be authentic. Come up with your own ideas, your own opinions, your own goals and your own identity. Who you are is what you believe in, what you choose to spend your energy on, who you choose to love and care for. You should never believe something just because someone told you to. You should never do something just because someone else did it. Find your own way. Follow your own inner voice. Focus on the things that get you fired up, that you feel passionate about, that breaks your heart or that makes you happy. Listen to yourself, not to the voice of others who have listened to themselves. Be the head, not the tail. In doing so, you will be less annoying, you will be more inspiring, you will be more satisfied, more proud of your results and more at peace.

CHAPTER EIGHT
Perfectionism

To be a perfectionist means you are someone who strives to be flawless. Perfectionists set such high expectations for themselves they cannot reach them - because a perfect human does not exist. Then when they don't reach their goals or standards, they're disappointed and unhappy with their results and themselves.

This doesn't sound like a satisfying, content life. Is it a choice?

As a child, I was a perfectionist. My Mum tells the story of when I wanted to join a calisthenics class. I was so excited. When I arrived, I could see some of the experienced members doing cartwheels and handstands. This was something I had never really attempted before, so I quickly tried it out. When I realised I couldn't do it, I broke down. My Mum tried to comfort me by explaining I was in the class to learn *how* to do those things and I didn't need to already know how to do it. There was no reasoning with me, in my mind I should have already been able to do them. I refused to join in on the class and never returned.

Chapter Eight: Perfectionism

I grew up as a perfectionist. I kept to my strengths, never really dabbling in sports or anything I thought I wouldn't excel in. I excluded myself from all classes and anything that involved me having to try too hard. If I couldn't already do it, I didn't bother. I didn't want to be vulnerable or bad at it, in fact I didn't even want to be average. It had nothing to do with anyone else, I didn't care if other people could do it. It wasn't because I was competitive in wanting to beat others, it was about me not allowing myself to fail.

In being a perfectionist, I robbed myself of so many opportunities to explore my options and I limited the person who I turned into.

My husband Dayna on the other hand, was an all-rounder. I met him while studying music. He wasn't the stereotypical musician who could only *just* do music. He was athletic, he loved playing basketball, footy and other sports. He could cook, dance, renovate houses and work on cars. He could listen and talk, he had a sense of humour and could be serious. He was so much more experienced than I was. I admired this so much about him, but it was so different to me that I struggled to understand him. He would want to do "fun" things with me, like play games or be active, and I would turn him down thinking they were anything but fun. I thought that sort of activity was silly and a waste of my time. I believed I was on a mission and every minute of my day should have been spent working towards my future, achieving my goals and striving for more (within my strengths of course). I didn't have time to waste on petty, little games. Gee, what a fun girlfriend I must have been!

Dayn is naturally so much more stable than me. He is balanced, content, at peace. I, on the other hand, am naturally un-balanced, discontent and hectic. Time keeps on ticking and I never have enough hours in the day to achieve my goals or live a life important enough. I'm always busy. So busy. Too busy. I've been exhausted a huge portion of my life because I just can't "be". I remember when we got engaged, my Dad described Dayn as the anchor, keeping the boat from getting lost at sea - and me? I was the crazy flag on top of the boat, going nuts.

The last few years I have been allowing my imperfections to surface. I want to relax, laugh more and be comfortable with myself, all of me, not just my strengths. I've learnt my weaknesses are also what makes me, *me*. I don't want to feel bad about myself. I've had enough of missing out on trying things for fear I won't be good enough and so I have been embracing my flaws.

I need to be deliberate about my thoughts. I need to remind myself that thoughts will come and go but they aren't always the whole truth. I need to swap the lies in my head about myself for the real stuff, things that are proven. I have to challenge myself regularly with doing things I don't think I can do and then if I fail, laugh and forget about it. When I say forget about it, I don't mean the experience magically vanishes from my memory. I mean, I have to choose not to repeat the thoughts or re-live the experience over and over again in my head. I need to trade those obsessive thoughts with other fun thoughts and good, healthy distractions. I surround myself with people who can support me in this. Luckily for me, I have a husband who is always willing to let me lose in all sorts of games. It has been a very therapeutic experience for both of us.

I realise, being busy does not make me more important. Being busy just means I miss out on other experiences and I'm often not fun to be around!

Chapter Eight: Perfectionism

If you can recognise you are a perfectionist and you're sick of it, make some different choices. Try out some of the things I mentioned. My default may always be striving for the best, but now I realise, I can control the level of 'perfectionism'. It can be a strength if it's in balance.

CHAPTER NINE
Vision

When my big brother was teaching me how to ride a bike, he forgot to give me one vital piece of information; where you look, is where you will end up. If I look to my right, I will naturally want to steer to my right. If my head is looking down at my legs, who knows where I'll end up? (Often on my face as I discovered!) If I look straight ahead - I will ride in a straight line. Ballerinas use a similar concept. When performing endless pirouettes, they keep their eyes on a spot so they are less likely to get dizzy and lose balance.

Once you realise you can act courageously even if you don't feel confident, you realise the truth about fame and people pleasing, you get prepared and flexible, gain perspective, change your judgements, ignore your feelings, find your own identity and let go of perfectionism, you will have a clearer picture of who you want to be and where you want to head. Focus on the details of that person. Meditate on the details. Choose to picture it in your head and then take steps that lead you to that life.

If I were to obsess over all of my weaknesses and the things I struggle with, I would find it hard to get where I want to be. That doesn't mean I need to be

Chapter Nine: Vision

ignorant or pretend I don't have weaknesses. I just know they're there, accept they're a part of me for now, realise it's a work in progress and then let it go. I regularly reshuffle my focus to the things I'm doing well and the progress I have made. In deciding to forgive myself, in being patient with myself and focusing on what I want from life, the weight of the load I am carrying lightens. I enjoy myself much more and things often fall into place.

I know this little book has been an absolute whirlwind. I recognise a lot of it may have been difficult to read and potentially you disagree with some of my ideas, but at least you have your very own opinion about it. Try to figure out why. This isn't a book to read once and let go of. Read it many times when you find yourself stuck in life, sitting in the one spot. Share the book with friends and family so you can have open discussions about your own opinions - ask them for their view. Come back to this book when you're feeling self-doubt, insecure and unsure of yourself. Constantly question who you are and why, then visualise yourself as the person you want to be.

Don't expect this book to change you. Don't think by reading more books like this, or by reading an extended version you'll be healed of your emotional dependancy, performance anxiety and fear. The words in this book may ring true, they may inspire, they may challenge, they may even educate you but the only way to actually grow and get out of your position is to *use* the words in this book and *do* things. Something. Anything! One step is better than none. Start with Chapter One. Come up with your own opinions, change your language and your thoughts. Be deliberate. This book was never meant to be *just* read, it was meant to be actioned and ultimately to assist you to get through what you're going through. Just like the aim of gaining a degree is to go and get the job, reading this book is meant to encourage you to step into the real world and into action.

Each chapter highlights my own personal revelations that have changed my life for the better. Sometimes it's been tough, but I'm achieving things I never thought I could. I'm sharing them with you because I believe they could change your life for the better too - but you must have your own personal revelations.

I'm a teacher because I love sharing what I know with others to see them develop, but just like I say to my students; I can't sing for you. I can give you the information, believe in you and encourage you but you must be the one to do the practice, figure out how to control your own instrument and sing! Now for you personally, the reader of this book; I know you can do this, but you must practice, figure out how to control your own mind and perform! These observations and experiences of mine cannot be yours - you have a different story to me, but hopefully they can trigger the truth or give you a prompt to help you write your own script.

Never give up.
Never think you have done all you can.
Never think your life is helpless or you are stuck being who you are.
There is always hope for something better.
Take up the challenge.
Perform.

www.ingramcontent.com/pod-product-compliance
Lightning Source LLC
LaVergne TN
LVHW042004060526
838200LV00041B/1877